Marriage LESSONS

Practical tips for a successful marriage

Wole & Dami
Olarinmoye

Dedication

We dedicate this book to our mothers, the late Mrs Victoria Ebun Olarinmoye and Mrs Rachael Wuraola Osajuyigbe. We thank God for your prayers, advice and guidance. We are forever in your debt.

To Mummy Aluko,

Thank you for your love,

wishing you all God's best in life

Love,

Wale + Jamie

xx

Marriage LESSONS

Practical tips for a successful marriage

Wole & Dami
Olarinmoye

WORD2PRINT
A Division of One-Touch Pro Ltd

MARRIAGE LESSONS

First published in the United Kingdom in 2016 by
Word2Print
www.word2print.com
ISBN: 978-1-908588-20-3

A CIP catalogue record for this title is available from the British Library

Printed by
Anthony Rowe Limited,
Wiltshire, England. UK

Design by Supreme Core Media
www.supremecoremedia.com

Contents

Foreword

We have both been passionate about marriage since we were young singles. One of the first things that we felt impressed on our hearts when we were courting, was that our marriage was to be a beacon of light to this generation. From that moment we felt it was important to do things properly so that in future we would be able to guide others the right way.

This book is a summary of the lessons we have learned in our marital journey. We have tried to list them in chronological order but we realise that no one learns these lessons completely at any stage. Learning in marriage is progressive but at certain times you become more aware of certain things than at other times.

Our hope is that you will learn these lessons quicker than we did and quickly enjoy the marital bliss that took us a few years to find.

God bless!
Wole and Dami

Introduction

How would you define a successful marriage? What makes a marriage successful? Would you describe your marriage as successful, convenient, satisfactory or even less? Is there something you can do to ensure a successful marriage? These and many other questions are constantly on the lips of single and married folk the world over. Is there an answer to failing marriages? Why is this important anyway?

In our opinion, every vice in society can be traced back to the failure of good strong families. A friend of ours who is a forensic psychiatrist has noted that in his various assessments of prison inmates, almost all of them have had significant family issues. At the heart of every family is a relationship between the parents. The state, condition and wellbeing of that relationship is shaping the children of our society and if we continue to get it wrong, we will continue to breed the miscreants, the criminals and the troublemakers of this world.

This book is our contribution to society and the world as a whole to say: "We can get it right in marriage and consequently in the family". Enough of broken homes and divorce. Enough of partnerships in which men and women have one foot in the door, exhibiting little commitment to each other. Enough of young ladies having several children for different men. These occurrences are damaging the mental health of our children. Damaged people damage other people; so this evil is self-perpetuating.

In writing this book, we are aware of the myriad of good books that have already been written on marriage. Our aim is to give you practical, personally tested advice and views, gleaned from our 18 years of marriage, which you can implement straightaway with great results.

Our hope, desire and prayer is that someone will read this book and take the decision to have a strong, successful, committed marriage relationship and thereby make a healthy contribution to society. They will also go on to have (if they so desire) well-balanced children who will go on to live well-balanced lives.

We wish you every blessing as you read.

Wole and Dami Olarinmoye
London, United Kingdom

Acknowledgments

We thank the Lord for the wisdom, desire and ability to write this book. Lord, without You we would not have been able to do this. Thank You.

We also thank the Marriage Enrichment Ministry of New Wine Church, London where we serve. We have learnt a lot just hanging around other couples who have also worked hard to develop beautiful marriages. We love you guys!

Our thanks also goes to Dr Muyiwa Olumoroti, our publisher, who keeps hounding us to write books and leave our mark in the sands of time. Thanks, bruv!

We also thank the editor, Karis Kayode Kolawole whose invaluable contribution has made this book the success story that it is. The Lord bless you real good.

Finally, we must thank all the lovely couples we have had the privilege of mentoring over the years. We have learnt so much from each of you and our marriage is stronger from knowing you. Thanks all!

1
Good Things Come to Those Who Wait

It's hard to wait around for something you know might never happen, but it's even harder to give up when you know it's everything you want. Author unknown

Dami

What are you looking for in a spouse?

No one is perfect but certain basic qualities or characteristics are essential. Before I met Wole, I was in a relationship for three years. Things appeared to be going well; I really loved and cared for him. I spent all my spare money on him, bought him gifts, did things for him and I was really happy doing all of that. I occasionally noticed he did nothing in return; never took me out, never bought me a birthday present, never bought me gifts. Admittedly he was not as well to do as I was at the time but 'never'?!

My mum was extremely concerned about our relationship. She told me a golden truth: 'The way a man treats you when you are courting will likely be the way he treats you when you are married". She said, "Even if he has very little or no money, if his heart is really with you, he will give you even the smallest of things". This chap never did.

In due course he called time on the relationship which really hurt considering all I had invested. He said he did not feel we were right for each other; it wasn't me, it was him and all the usual excuses that people come up with when they want to move on from a relationship for no good reason. I pleaded with him, I cried for days because it hurt so much. I did not want the pain or stigma of a broken relationship. I was a good Christian girl; I didn't plan for this. I already had my life planned out with him from my teenage years. I didn't want to be seen as moving from one relationship to another. So many different thoughts crowded my mind all at the same time.

It was not easy to get over. I prayed and prayed for nights on end to get rid of the pain. After about six months of struggling with my emotions, I eventually realised I was holding him in unforgiveness. By holding onto the hurt, I was further harming myself and my emotions. I realised that this would probably affect how I viewed men and would likely affect my next relationship; so, I made the very difficult decision to forgive him. I would not hold it against him. I prayed for all the pain, bitterness and hurt to be taken away. I made up my mind to walk in love towards him as I would to any other person and that was how I received my freedom.

At that point I made up my mind that I would wait for the right person to come along. Having experienced what I did not want in a relationship, I became fairly clear about what I wanted. I made a little list for myself and decided I would wait till 'he' came along.

This was my list. I wanted a man that was:

- Spiritually inclined
- Purpose driven
- Professionally established (or at least on the way)
- Physically attractive
- Mentally intelligent
- Marriage material (homely)
- Decent family background
- Friendship material

Do you notice how even before I met Wole, I was already thinking in line with the Decasections of Life? If you haven't heard about the Decasections, you need to read our other book called 'The Decasections of Life: the ultimate manual for living the balanced life'.

Now let me explain my list in turn:

Spiritually inclined: I wanted someone who shared my spiritual values in life. I believe in having a good relationship with God my Maker and I have been like that for most of my life. Getting involved with someone who shared my values would mean we could grow together spiritually. It would also mean we would have similar reference points in case of disputes. I wanted someone who valued the Bible as the word of God as I do. He would be someone who valued my chastity as I did as I had made up my mind not to have sex before marriage. He would be someone who believed in having a good character, being nice and kind, a gentleman in attitude and disposition.

Purpose driven: I was looking for someone who had an idea of what he wanted from life. He didn't have to have it all figured out, but he had to have some direction. Although I believe we all have a grand design for our lives, he didn't necessarily have to be someone who had it all completely laid out (we were still young) but he had to have a sense of purpose.

Professionally established: You might have noticed there was nothing about money, a car or a big house on my list. That's not because it was not important. I do like the good things of life like most women do. Maybe even more! However, at our young age in our early 20s, I was not expecting someone who had it all lined up. I wanted someone with whom we could grow together financially. It was important though that he had to be established or on the way to being established professionally. If he had a decent vocation or profession of some kind, the rest would fall into place.

Physically attractive: I certainly wanted a man who would not only be attractive to me but also would find me attractive. Not everyone will get a George Clooney or a David Beckham, but if you wrinkle your nose in disgust every time you see your spouse, it's not looking too good for your relationship! Likewise if he cannot bear to look at you but thinks you are a great person, he might end up looking at someone else (or being with someone else) while he is with you. Attraction is an individual thing but it should be there in some way.

Mentally intelligent: I am a quick thinker, able to juggle two or three things at a time. I can easily multi-task, so a man who is slow will frustrate me. He didn't have to have the IQ of a rocket scientist but he had to be sharp, a quick thinker, someone who is ahead of the game.

Marriage material: Not all good men are marriage material or ready to settle down. Some are happy to be eternal boyfriends keeping their options open. Once talk of settling down surfaces on the agenda, they are on the way out. Even when such men eventually settle down, they will always refer back to and long for their lives as single men. I wanted a man who was homely, willing and ready to settle and have a family at the right time.

Family background: This may not seem too important now but many years ago for a young girl of African origin, it was of great importance. Even now it is very significant. Certain things run in families. If his dad was a womaniser, chances are he could be too. If his parents had a terrible marriage, chances are he would too. When you get married to a man, you not only marry him but his family and especially his mum too! (The mum-in-law situation!)

Friendship material: I wanted to marry a man who would be my best friend. Many young ladies miss it at this point. They have a guy who is their close friend but they feel unable to commit to him in marriage as they are waiting for some Prince Charming to ride out of the clouds and sweep them off their feet. Wake up ladies! That is fairy tale stuff! You want a man who will be your friend. Someone you can hang out with and chat with on the phone for hours and not get bored. Someone you can be with doing nothing because you are comfortable with each other. This is extremely important. We often speak to a number of ladies who say things like: 'I cannot marry him, he is my friend, and we know each other too well'. Hello! That is the whole point of marriage - knowing each other very well!

So, armed with a clear list, it was easy to see who did not fit the bill. There were certain men I would not even consider as they failed on the first and most important point for me (spiritual). There was one particular guy who was obsessed with me. He came round to see me at work almost on a daily basis. He was financially loaded! He also had a decent family background BUT he could not keep it in his pants! Ticked many points but failed crucial ones:

- He did not share my spiritual values (although he promised to attend church with me!)

- He was very arrogant and wanted me to feel privileged he was interested in me. (I sensed a domineering man and an abusive relationship!)

- He was definitely NOT marriage material; he had been through some of my colleagues (sexually) and many others in town. (I sense a heartbreaker and an unfaithful man!)

- He was not my type of friend as he was always boasting about some professional or sexual achievement. So there was no way I could consider him.

There was another guy who was interested. Nice chap, good spiritual and moral values, financially loaded but we just didn't hit it off on the friendship level. Conversation was very forced and we just didn't flow.

Follow your trained heart

I used the phrase 'trained heart' but others prefer the term 'hunch' or 'intuition'. If you have not practiced following your heart or your 'hunches', then when choosing a spouse is not the first time to test it out. If you have and you know what works for you, then following your heart opens you to a world of leading, direction and guidance that you cannot explain or access with your five senses. I believe the main way to train your heart is learning to become more spiritual and testing out your 'heart tugs' to see where they lead you. I believe God is able to guide you to what belongs to you, beyond what you can see, feel or know. Start out with matters of little importance before you start to take life-changing decisions based on intuition.

Steve Jobs said:

> *"Your time is limited, so don't waste it living someone else's life. Don't be trapped by dogma - which is living with the results of other people's thinking. Don't let the issue of others opinions drown out your own inner voice. And most important, have the courage to follow your heart and intuition. They somehow already know what you truly want to become. Everything else is secondary."*

As part of my professional development, I decided to

study midwifery after finishing my training as a nurse. I had already gained admission to one institution but I felt very uncomfortable about my admission there. I felt my heart being tugged in a different direction. As I said earlier, I believe in following my heart. Whatever your religious persuasion, I believe God always wants the best for us and He guides us through our hearts. If you learn to follow your heart, you will access many things that will otherwise not be obvious to you.

I felt my heart strings being tugged towards studying my midwifery at another institution. I sought admission there and on arrival, I picked up the very last application form. On the day of my interview, things did not go too well but I was given admission to the college anyway. I was later told by a tutor that I was picked only because they felt there was something special about me, not because of my performance on the day. It was at this college I met Wole.

He was a medical student at the time and I got to know him through the college Christian fellowship. Although he seemed quite distant initially, we gradually got to know each other as we had the same friends. He loved listening to me talk (I can talk!) and initially he said very little. He always seemed happy to see me and our friendship blossomed. As I got to know him better, he certainly ticked every single box on my list which further confirmed things for me. All our friends were getting into formal relationships but we stayed just friends.

Wole eventually left medical school and started working as a doctor in another town. Although we maintained contact by letter (this was before emails and mobile phones), he still did not make any moves. I had many other offers in that time but none of the chaps fully ticked the boxes for me as Wole did.

Take the decision to wait

At some point I had to take a decision: go with what was available or wait for the man of my dreams. I chose to wait as Wole was still available. I have seen over the years, the downside of people going with what is available, just for the sake of getting married. The pain and cost of a bad relationship far outweighs the glamour of being married. I remember a lady who had her heart broken just before she was due to get married. The relationship was called off and she was devastated. Within a few months she was in another relationship and shortly after that they were married. The marriage did not last a year. It was what we call a rebound relationship in which a person jumps into a relationship to compensate for the loss of a previous one. Relationships like those rarely work out well as the premise of the relationship is usually not pure.

It took two years for Wole to come round to propose but he was well worth the wait. In that time I had other decisions to make. My ex-boyfriend had returned realising he made an error and wanted to come back. I had to decide whether to return to what I was familiar with but inadequate, or value myself enough to wait for someone who valued and appreciated me for who I was. Again I chose to wait. I had clearly seen what I did not want in a relationship; why go back to being unhappy? Loneliness is a bad thing and this drives many people into relationships they know are bad for them but is it really worth the pain and heartache?

I would like to encourage ladies out there who feel they have been waiting a long time. They are worried about their ticking biological clocks, worried that everyone else seems to be getting hooked up, worried that they are being left behind. In my role counselling and supporting women, I have been exposed to the experiences of those in unhappy relationships. As a result I have come to the conclusion that the pain, heartache and strain of an unhappy relationship is not worth it especially when you are walking into it knowing that there will be potential problems. There is someone out there who appreciates you for who you are, not just for what you can offer physically or otherwise. Value yourself enough to wait for the right person. It is always well worth the wait.

As you continue reading this book, you will see a number of things you should be doing in your waiting period before your ideal man comes along.

I must emphasise a note of caution at this point. Do not take any major decision on a whim saying, "it felt right in my heart". No! That's why I have intentionally used the phrase 'trained heart'. Many ladies get into relationships that end up being toxic using that same phrase, "it felt right". A trained heart would be able to differentiate between plain infatuation and actual substance. If you are unsure, use the list I have provided to assess your 'target'. Does he tick the boxes or is he just a pretty face with money?

Chapter lessons:

- Good things come to those who wait. Be patient and

  Don't settle for less than you deserve.

- Don't allow yourself to be treated less than you deserve by anyone.

- If you have concerns about anything in your relationship, do not progress to marriage until they have been satisfactorily resolved. Every couple with marriage problems we have counselled, showed clear signs which started during courtship.

- Have clear desires on what you want in a spouse.

- Train your heart to follow your God ordained purpose.

- Learn to follow your trained heart; intuition is a powerful thing but don't take any major decisions on a whim.

- Take the decision to wait for the right person.

2
Preparation is the Key to Success

Before anything else, preparation is the key to success.
Alexander Graham Bell
The most important thing in marriage is being the right person;
the second is marrying the right person.
Wole Olarinmoye

Wole

Marriage is a venture, a vocation, an undertaking, an endeavour even. To practice as a professional in any field of endeavour, you need to be trained. Once you have been trained and qualified, you will probably be required to maintain your registration with continuous professional development (CPD) in order to remain relevant and up to date.

When it comes to relationships and marriage, people expect to see someone, fall in love and live happily ever. They get surprised when they have arguments, conflict and disagreements; and if they feel their differences are 'irreconcilable' they end the relationship and move on to someone else only to repeat the process. Unfortunately in that time, children may have arrived and things get complicated. There is no training, no supervision, no mentoring. Can you imagine a surgeon who decides to teach himself how to perform surgery? What about a mechanic who decides to teach himself about fixing cars? They might well learn something through trial and error but what about the damage that would have been caused along the way?

Some people eventually get it right in relationships. They finally settle down after serial dating, broken hearts and bad experiences. Unfortunately children are sometimes caught up in all of this. Before going into ANY relationship especially one building up to marriage, there should be a significant element of preparation to avoid all the unnecessary heartache that is often encountered.

Every failed relationship will leave you with scars. The more serious the relationship, the more serious the scars. These scars have a way of adversely influencing your next relationship and the more of these scars you have, the more adverse the influence.

Many years ago, when I started to consider relationships and marriage, I began to 'extend my radar' in search of THE ONE. I was lining up my choices and praying about them intensely when I felt an inspirational message in my heart: *You are not ready for marriage.* Remember Dami discussed 'following your trained heart' in the previous chapter. This shocked me initially. How could I not be ready for marriage? I was in medical school heading towards being a doctor and I was a nice person in my opinion. How could I not be ready? But as I started to reflect more on this, I realised the only way I could be ready for marriage, was to be prepared for marriage. The only way to avoid the pain and heartache many often encounter is to be *maritally* trained. In other words, I needed to go through some form of preparation in order to be ready for marriage.

In my reflection, I have identified three forms of preparation necessary to get ready for marriage.

1. Spiritual preparation

2. Psychological preparation

3. Physical preparation

I will discuss each in turn and you will see how it all fits in to preparing you for marriage.

Spiritual preparation

Now don't switch off on me because I have mentioned spiritual preparation. It's not some 'mumbo jumbo'. Whatever your faith or religion, whatever your conviction or persuasion, whatever your beliefs or opinions, spiritual preparation is required for a successful marriage. This is the reason why:

15

The most important thing in marriage is being the right person; the second is marrying the right person.

So at this point we will ask some very pertinent questions: Who are you exactly? Who do people think you are? But maybe the most important question of these should be: Who are you supposed to be?

In my book, *The Decasections of Life,* I dealt with whole concept of identity. If you do not know who you are exactly, and even more importantly who you are supposed to be, then you are at risk of having an identity crisis. If you are in such a position and do not know who you are, how can you make a relationship work or even more accurately how can you choose the right spouse for yourself? From the series of questions above, there are at least three people who claim to be you:

Person 1: The person that others see

Person 2: The real person behind the façade

Person 3: The person you are supposed to be

In any close relationship, and most especially in marriage, your spouse will be exposed to all three versions of you. Your spouse could possibly marry the person he or she thought you were, whom he or she had fallen in love with but then progressively discovers the real person behind the façade who he or she might totally detest. For example, a lady falls in love with a handsome, popular member of the community who appears to be a total gentleman. Deep down though he is a misogynist who has very little regard for women, seeing them simply as tools for his own gratification. Although she wants a wholesome marriage relationship, he only wants a trophy wife and a sex toy. While they were courting, he made certain remarks which alerted her to his true nature but she kept telling herself 'not to be silly'. He was quite domineering and bullying but she explained it away as his 'strong personality'. They get married and immediately start having problems. Communication is forced as he thinks she is beneath him. Sex is forced as he thinks she owes it to him. When sex is not forthcoming as readily as he demands, he looks for it elsewhere.

What went wrong? **There was no spiritual preparation.** The young lady got married to Person 1 (whom she thought he was) only for Person 2 (who he really is) to show up. Person 2 was always going to make an appearance as that is his true nature, so the marriage ends up on the rocks. Adequate spiritual preparation on her part would have helped her to recognise her true value and self-worth, and she would have refused to be treated any less than she should. The marriage would not have gone ahead if she had insisted on being treated as an equal. We deal with this more in the chapter titled 'Marriage is for Both of Us'.

Misogyny which is defined as dislike of, contempt for, or ingrained prejudice against women has been used in the example above but it could be any vice that defines you like extreme anger, financial impropriety, gambling, lying, stealing, drugs, alcohol, just to name a few. If you have stuff in your life that has not been dealt with, then you are in need of spiritual preparation. Every great man or woman who has fallen from grace in history has done so due to a significant disparity between Person 1 and 2, the person that others see and the real person behind the mask. Hidden secrets will eventually be revealed.

Your mission (should you choose to accept it) is to make all three versions of you as close as is feasibly possible, such that the person you portray is actually the person you are while working towards becoming the person you are supposed to be.

When you are the right person, it becomes easier to attract the right person for you. Many of you reading this book may already be married. Your spouse knows you as Person 1 (the person people think you are) and may only have had glimpses of your Person 3 (the person you are supposed to be). It is never too late for spiritual preparation. We are by no means suggesting you attain a state of perfection in character or life before you marry but it is important that you work towards being the best version of your true self. Remember that being the right person is the real work. You cannot change anyone else but you can work on yourself and be a better person. If there are aspects of your true nature that you need to hide away from people especially your spouse or spouse to be, then you are in need of spiritual preparation.

We are told that in the Garden of Eden, Adam and Eve were both naked and unashamed. This indicates openness which is a core requirement for a successful marriage. If you cannot be open with your spouse or spouse to be, then you are projecting Person 1 (who people think you are) and hiding away Person 2 (the real you when nobody is looking). This means your spouse is married to a false person, not the real you. That in itself is a recipe for future problems.

Psychological preparation

Many people are not psychologically prepared for the impact that marriage will have on their lives. It is a totally new world. In fact, the longer you have been single, the more difficult it is to adapt to the married life. Marriage can feel intrusive, invasive, uncomfortable, meddling and you need to be properly psychologically prepared for it.

You might wonder why I have used the term 'properly'. It is because we have all already been prepared for marriage in one way or another. You already have certain views and opinions. You have already made certain unconscious choices and you are already heading down certain paths in life as a whole. The bad news for many of us is that we have been wrongly prepared. Our views on relationships and marriage are warped by what we saw or didn't see in our parents, what we see on TV, the big screen, previous experiences, female periodicals, lads' publications and opinions from friends. We could go on and on.

Views like 'men are only after one thing' or 'women only want your money' are very pervasive in society. Views such as 'marriage was not designed to last', 'marriage is a trap', 'men or women from certain places will never make good spouses' are also among the lies that have been peddled down the generations. Don't imbibe those lies! Marriage is supposed to be sweet. It was designed to be beautiful. You are right to want a blissful happy marriage because that is how it should be but it won't come cheap. You have to prepare for it.

The truth is, Prince Charming and Princess Bella only exist in fairy tales. No one is coming to sweep you off your feet. Stars will not appear before your eyes when you meet her or him for the first time. If you have any such experiences, it is likely to be infatuation with a tinge of lust; pure and simple. Without adequate preparation you are not likely to live happily ever after.

We need proper psychological preparation in order to prepare for marriage. Benjamin Franklin said, "By failing to prepare, you are preparing to fail." We need to prepare for differences in lots of areas. Let me name a few:

1. Gender differences: Men and women are very different. We think differently, act differently, and see things differently. Nuff said!

2. Spiritual differences (beliefs and attitudes to God)

3. Cultural differences (beliefs and attitudes due to culture)

4. Family background differences (upbringing)

5. Financial differences (spending and saving)

6. Personality differences (who we are; for example, introvert versus extrovert)

7. Recreational differences ('Mrs Eating Out' versus 'Mr Holiday Abroad')

8. Sex drive differences

9. Ambition differences

10. Intellectual differences

Some of these possible differences are so important to you as a person that you will feel you cannot compromise on them. It would be silly to start a relationship with someone who has significantly different views on something that holds great importance for you. Some other differences may not be as important and you may need to be prepared to compromise as your spouse may have different opinions on how things are done. Different is not necessarily wrong, just different. Unfortunately different is what causes arguments which can lead to rifts.

Part of your psychological preparation is for you to understand what is important to you as a person and what is not so important. When I was preparing myself psychologically, I noticed some gaping holes. I didn't really know much about women with respect to behaviour, thinking or attitudes. I had not read any books on marriage. I had not attended any seminars on relationships. I did not have many close female friends. Simply put, I WAS NOT PREPARED!

There I was, looking to make one of the greatest decisions of my life and I was about to take the step not knowing anything of importance about what I was about to do! Can you imagine investing all your savings on the stock market without doing any research into the product or the company you are investing in? That is exactly what we do when we start relationships without adequate preparation. So I started to read books and attend seminars. I asked intelligent questions about women and developed some wonderful friendships which served as a learning resource for me. I am so grateful for the lady friends I was blessed with. I realised that many of them came into my life or became closer after I realised I was not ready for marriage. Little things like commenting on new hairdos, appreciating nice outfits, noticing when they are upset and caring enough to ask if they are okay were tips I picked up from my friends which I still use till this day in my marriage.

Physical preparation

This is somewhat straightforward. This has to do with your physical appearance. We are by no means advocating that anyone gets married or stays married based on physical appearance alone, but you do need to be attractive to your spouse. So a bit of effort in this area will always be highly appreciated.

The contents of this chapter apply to those who are already married as much as those who are yet to marry. You still need to continue your *spiritual* preparation, your *psychological* preparation and certainly your *physical* preparation. We are not perfect and we need to keep working at the people we *are*, while becoming the people we are supposed to be, the best versions of ourselves.

Chapter lessons:

- Even in marriage, preparation is the key to success.

- Preparation should be spiritual, psychological and physical.

- Every failed relationship leaves you with a scar.

- The most important thing in marriage is being the right person.

3

Marriage is for Both of Us

Two are better than one for they can help each other succeed.
The Preacher

Wole

This is going to sound strange and maybe a bit obvious but this is a very important lesson in marriage. There are two people involved in a marriage relationship. Marriage is therefore for both of us.

Before I got married, I had made up my mind to be the best husband in the world. I had heard phrases like 'Happy wife, happy life' and I determined that my wife would be happy. To me, that meant agreeing with everything my wife wanted and said. To help you understand this, let me introduce you to my wife. Dami is a strong-willed, focussed and organised woman who has her whole life planned and laid out before her. She knows what she wants specifically in every situation.

25

She wakes up knowing what she wants to eat that day and has a plan for each and every day right down to the last detail. She is 'organisation' personified. I am more laid back, easy going, not too worried about the small print as long as the main things are in place. Very contrasting personalities!

For the first two years of our marriage, I agreed with everything she said and did everything she wanted but inside I was beginning to get frustrated. Now, Dami is a very good woman. I am fortunate and very blessed to have her in my life. Many women are good but I truly believe there is no woman like her. She excels most women in every department and cumulatively she is head and shoulders above all others. I have never wished I were married to anyone else and that is unlikely to EVER change but her desires are HER desires. The things she likes are the things SHE likes. The things she wants are the things SHE wants. I did not particularly desire, want or like the same things and my self-imposed lack of expression or involvement was beginning to frustrate me.

Frustration can only be suppressed for so long and one day it all erupted. As we resolved things I realised my error. I had removed one whole person from the marriage equation - Me. I had given Dami the wrong impression, making her feel like I agreed with everything she expressed when deep down I had my own opinions, desires and views on things. I had taken 'Mr Nice Guy' to the extreme. We learnt the vital marriage lesson:

Marriage is for both of us.

It is no longer a proper marriage if only one person is happy.

Being a good husband or wife does not mean suppressing your opinion. In fact it cannot be said that you have properly agreed on a subject if one person has hidden or failed to express their true opinion about an issue.

Marriage is not about suppression or domination. It is about each spouse feeling valued enough to express themselves without the fear of feeling judged. It takes two to tango effectively.

In my case I held back until I exploded. I had suppressed myself. In other relationships what occurs is not suppression but domination; one spouse imposing themselves against the will of the person they are married to. Whenever there is an imbalance in a relationship, problems are likely to occur.

Now although there was no abuse in our situation, there was a relationship imbalance. What happened to us could easily have become an abusive relationship in which one person starts to take advantage of the other's good nature or less confrontational nature. Both domination and suppression will have significant negative effects. These are explained further below.

Suppression wanting to avoid confrontation

Although not a form of abuse, there is a definite relationship imbalance. I found myself in this situation in which I just wanted to please my wife so I avoided any form of dispute even over simple choices. Below are some scenarios we could find ourselves in that would reflect this type of suppression.

Scenario 1
She says: "What colour curtains should we buy? I like the yellow ones"
Me externally: "That's fine Honey"
Me internally: "The yellow curtains won't go with the furniture but I'm not going to point that out; can't be bothered to argue"

Scenario 2
She says: "The green carpet looks unique, what do you think?"
Me externally: "I agree sweetheart'"
Me internally: "Green! Is she bananas?!"

Scenario 3
She says: "I was thinking about buying a pram and a Moses basket for the baby but I'm not sure we can afford it. What do you think?"
Me externally: "Whatever you decide darling"
Me internally: "If you cannot see that we can't afford it, that's up to you!"

No one can keep up that type of attitude. It is artificial and fake. Communication is the life blood of any relationship and if you cannot discuss simple things or even have amicable disagreements, then your marriage will not thrive very well.

Suppression due to inferiority

This is a very common form of abuse in marriage. It is a situation in which a spouse feels inferior for whatever reason, which can also encourage abuse. Many feel inferior due to less privileged backgrounds, financial dependence, mental health problems like depression, physical disability, previous negative relationships, insecurity issues and so forth. The obvious imbalance here opens up the relationship to possible abuse. It is important that spouses make each other feel comfortable despite obvious disparities.

I will use financial dependence as an example. There will always be some disparity in earning amongst couples. Some ladies earn less than their husbands due to working part time or not working at all while caring for children. As a result, they may feel less entitled to the family income, as they did not directly earn it. However, it is the responsibility of the higher earning spouse (in this case the man) to make his wife feel comfortable enough to discuss the family's finances as an equal even though she did not directly contribute to it.

When we got married, we agreed that we would

jointly own everything including money. So although I may earn more, Dami has as much right to the money as I do. It would be wrong for either of us to take a unilateral decision on what we both own without prior agreement as it belongs to both of us. Let us not forget that money is not the only factor in a relationship. The lower earning spouse may contribute to the family in other ways such as childcare, housework, and emotional warmth which cannot be financially quantified.

Another example could be physical disability. Here are a few scenarios:

Jack and Jill have been married two years. They have a one year old-son. Jill is disabled with back pain from an accident and suffers from bouts of depression due to her condition. She is unable to work but keeps the house spic and span and looks after her husband and son very well. Below are examples of conversations between them:

Conversation 1

Jack: "We need new carpets, this one is quite old. What do you think?"

Jill: "You earn the money sweetheart, you should decide".

Jack: "I might earn the money dear, but it belongs to both of us so we both need to agree on what to do".

In this scenario, Jill feels inferior as she does not earn

the money but Jack takes the right steps to redress the relationship imbalance and thereby making Jill feel loved and respected.

Conversation 2

Jack: "I feel like going out tonight, where should we go?"

Jill: "My back is playing up again. I am always preventing you from having a good time. Why don't you go ahead and enjoy yourself, don't worry about me."

Jack: "Don't be silly sweetie, I married you and your back. I love you anyway. We'll order a takeaway and rent a nice movie. That way we'll both enjoy ourselves."

In this scenario, Jill feels inferior due to her bad back always playing up. Jack reassures her and takes the right steps to redress the relationship imbalance, and thereby making Jill feel loved and secure.

Whatever the source of inferiority, it is the responsibility of the unaffected spouse to provide the relevant and required support to avoid the relationship being imbalanced. This would involve constant reassurance and certainly, never using the weakness of a spouse against them.

Domination

This is also a very common form of abuse in marriage. Whenever a spouse feels he or she has the right to dominate the other, this will always result in an abusive relationship. All forms of abuse arise from one person feeling superior to the other and invariably acting it out.

My advice to anyone who finds themselves in the position of the abuser is this: 'Think about what you are doing'. No one is more important than another. It doesn't matter how much you earn, what you do as a job or how well known you are; that does not give you the right to abuse anyone. Be nice! It actually feels nice to be nice. Pride and arrogance go before a fall so humble yourself. Accept your own humanity and stop lording it over your spouse. If you have lost yourself to physical abuse in your marriage then I encourage you to seek help. There is no place for violence in marriage. In fact there is no place for abuse of any kind in a marital union.

My advice to anyone who finds themselves in the position of the 'abused' is this: 'You deserve better'. No one has the right to treat you like dirt. You are worth more than that. The basic problem for many who are being abused is inferiority complex. Unfortunately this means that many who are being abused invite the abuse on themselves by the way they see themselves. You are likely to be seen the way you see yourself and you are likely to be treated the way you treat yourself. You are a priceless gem! Value yourself, and don't accept negative treatment from anyone.

Who is in charge of the marriage?

This is the question that usually results in domination or suppression. The common thinking is that someone needs to be in a particular position to have the final answer or to settle disputes. The traditional model over the centuries had the man in charge. In charge as the provider, protector, policy maker, king of the household. His word was law. The woman was only to provide the satisfaction of appetites (culinary and sexual) and to have children.

In more modern times with women assuming a more prominent role in society, the traditional roles have been blurred. It is not uncommon to have men staying at home with the children while the woman goes out to work. It is more common to have shared roles where both spouses work and share the house work equally or in some proportion depending on how much work each person is doing.

Most women are natural home makers. They naturally default to caring for the home, looking after the children and making sure things run smoothly on the domestic front. Most men are natural hunters. They default to provision, making money for the household and providing security for the family.

In our 'learning to tango' as a couple, we realised that in marriage, it is probably best that you should fulfil a role that comes naturally or easily to you otherwise you will get stressed and frustrated in the relationship. You will start to resent your spouse and this can lead to conflict. Dami is very house proud. It upsets her if the house is untidy or in a mess so it never is! Our house is like a show home. She is also a very doting mother. The children must eat well, dress well and be well behaved at all times. When she was working full time, she was unable to fully do the things that came naturally to her and she became very stressed. She got upset with me for not helping enough. She got upset with those we hired to clean as they were not doing it well enough so we had to have a 'round table conference' to sort things out.

Since it comes naturally to me to work hard and earn a living for the family, we agreed that I would work a little more and she would work a little less. We agreed that working full time was not very compatible with her looking after the house and the children. This is also very hard work by the way! By working part time, she had more time do things we had previously contracted out, like ironing, gardening and cleaning which she now did on her days off. She was no longer stressed and frustrated, I could do some extra work to make up the income loss and everyone was happy! In fact, reducing the amount of work we were contracting out also saved us money.

In our 'learning to tango' as a couple, we learnt a very important lesson here: a good marriage is complementary. We deal with this in a bit more detail later but suffice it to say that what comes naturally to me should fill in for what does not come naturally to you and vice versa.

I must add a caveat here: not all relationships will fit into this mould. Some men are house-husbands looking after the children as they find that it is more financially viable for the women to work. Some men might be very good in housework and should not allow the traditional roles to stop their involvement. The couple should agree on what works best for them.

Going back to the issue of who is in charge, many people blame the Bible and the church for the whole concept of submission. 'Women must submit to men' and this has caused a lot of dispute in relationships. Some men have even used this as an excuse to dominate their women! I want to clarify this so let us look at the Bible passage where it is written;

> *And further, submit to one another out of reverence for Christ. For wives, this means submit to your husbands as to the Lord. For a husband is the head of his wife as Christ is the head of the church. He is the Saviour of his body, the church. As the church submits to Christ, so you wives should submit to your husbands in everything. For husbands, this means love your wives, just as Christ loved the church. He gave up his life for her to make her holy and clean, washed by the cleansing of God's word.*

Ephesians 5:21-26 from the New Living Translation.

Many are quick to point out the part in verse 22 that

says wives should submit to their husbands. Please back up a little to verse 21. It starts off by saying 'SUBMIT TO ONE ANOTHER!!!' Yes, it does say that wives should submit or give the husband the final say but it also says husbands should love their wives as Christ loved the church and GAVE UP HIS LIFE FOR HER. Any man that wants his wife to submit to him unreservedly should be prepared to love her unreservedly to the point of giving up his life for her. It should show in the things he does for her on a daily basis.

Yes, I believe the man should lead his home. There is enough evidence in society showing that the 'Absent Father Syndrome' is probably one of the greatest social crisis facing humanity at the moment, BUT the only man who qualifies to lead his home and to have his wife submit to him is the man who loves his wife to the point of giving up his life for her. You cannot expect your wife to submit to you unconditionally if you are not loving her unconditionally.

So the real issue is not one of 'who is in charge?' but how are we individually fulfilling our roles in this marital relationship? This throws up many pertinent questions:

- Do we have specified roles in our relationship?

- Do we have 'job descriptions' for what we do?

- Do we stick to our roles and perform our job descriptions?

- Are we just harping along hoping it all works out leaving things to chance or are we being deliberate and intentional about making sure things run on rails?

- Who should take the lead to make sure the bills are paid? It should be whoever is better with money, saving money, not spending money.

- Who should take the lead to make sure the house is well maintained? It should be whoever is better with cleaning and tidying up.

- Who should take the lead in providing for the family? It should be whoever has the better earning potential.

These points do not mean that you play no role if you are not taking the lead. You both work together but for effectiveness, one spouse has oversight of the area they are better equipped in dealing with.

The other question to ask is: Are you doing all you reasonably can to play your part? The argument a lot of women put forward is that their husbands are not fit to lead or not equipped to give direction as the head. I agree with you. Many are not. We have not all come from the right backgrounds and as we dealt with in previous chapters, we have not all had the right preparation required.

For married couples our advice is this: let us help each other to develop the necessary traits and attributes required to be all we should be. This is exemplified by the story of a mayor's wife who stopped to talk to a labourer on the road side while on a state visit with her husband. She spent quite a few minutes chatting with him and afterwards her husband asked who he was. 'That was the man I almost married' she said. The mayor looking smug smiled saying, 'Aren't you glad you married me instead? You wouldn't be the wife of a mayor today'. She smiled back at him and retorted, 'Actually if I had married him, he would be the mayor today'.

Go through the questions we have asked together and arrive at some sort of structure and plan that will help your marriage run smoothly without domination, suppression or inferiority.

For single ladies our advice is this: Do not marry a man who you feel is not competent enough to lead you into the future you desire. It will only lead to frustration. For single men our advice is this: Do not marry a woman you feel will not accept your leadership and love.

Chapter lessons:

- Marriage is for BOTH of us. We are BOTH supposed to be happy and fulfilled in this marriage.

- A good marriage is complementary.

- Submission works both ways!

- Do what comes naturally to you and complement each other.

4
The Best Things in Life are Free

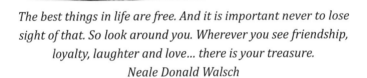

The best things in life are free. And it is important never to lose sight of that. So look around you. Wherever you see friendship, loyalty, laughter and love... there is your treasure.
Neale Donald Walsch

Wole

I first heard the above saying while I was in medical school. I was sitting in a urology lecture on acute urinary retention. This is a condition which usually occurs in men due to an enlargement of the prostate, a tiny structure at the base of the bladder. It gets bigger in men with age and can obstruct the flow of urine resulting in urinary retention. While describing the condition, my consultant acted out how a man with acute urinary retention would present. He told us very few things beat the feeling of going to toilet, whipping it out (or sitting down as the case may be) and just letting it flow, especially if you had been holding it in for a while. He concluded his example by saying, 'the best things in life are free'.

Dami and I were both in our mid-twenties when we got married. We didn't have a house to our name. In fact our entire possessions fit into two large suitcases! We had just returned to the UK and our first place was a one bed flat above a convenience store in East London. As a result, we had 'pets' who shared the place with us; little furry animals with long tails. Rats to be precise!

We had only one electric heater in the house and we would carry it from the bedroom to the bathroom or sitting room. I remember that we had to be in the same room at all times since there was only one heater. But in all of that, the really interesting thing is that we were happy. We didn't notice so much what we didn't have because we had each other. We couldn't see so much what we didn't have because we were so satisfied with what we did have. We were so happy.

We spent our first wedding anniversary walking around a park in Stratford, East London, holding hands, chatting and just gazing into each other's eyes. We were really happy.

Today, we are a million miles away from those days in terms of status, possessions, achievement and location but we are not any happier than we were then. We now have children, high flying careers, can afford more, go on more expensive holidays, give each other lavish gifts on our birthdays and anniversaries but we are not any happier than we were in those days. Over the years, we have learnt a very valuable life and marriage lesson: the best things in life are free.

Neale Donald Walsch says never lose sight of the fact that the best things in life cost little or no money. We were on a couple's retreat a few weeks before I wrote this chapter and someone asked the question in our open forum: 'How do you keep romance alive in your marriage?' Lots of answers were given but the best one for me was this: 'What did you do when romance was alive? Go back to those things'.

For us, our relationship and marriage was built on friendship, love, romance and loyalty. Our being happy was not based on what we had or didn't have. It was based on our being content with each other. We have all heard that money doesn't buy happiness. It's true. I use this reference a lot but unfortunately they are a case in point. Look at famous celebrities; they are some of the most unhappy people in the world. They have and own everything we could ever want but most of them are not happy. They move from high profile relationship to high profile relationship, get involved in drugs and alcohol, and check in and out of rehab-which just reinforces this vital marriage lesson: the best things in life are free.

Money has a place

Money is important. It is the currency by which we live in this day and age. We need it to eat, clothe, school, live and pretty much do everything. We are not advocating that you live like hermits, but we are also clearly stating that having plenty of money will not make you happier. It should not be the focus of your life and certainly not the focus of your marriage. Gareth Brooks said,

> *"You aren't wealthy until you have something that money cannot buy".*

I make my next point at the risk of sounding a little macabre or frightening. At the point of death, no one thinks about making more money or having more stuff. No one at the point of death wished they could close one more business deal or take over one more corporation. All we think about are our relationships and purpose. During the September 11, 2001 terrorist attacks in America, most of those who thought they were going to die had one overriding thought in their minds - family and relationships. Many of them made calls and left messages. At the point of death, we think about those we love and those we will leave behind; the things we did and especially the things we should have done. I have decided in advance not to die with any regrets, so that means treasuring and nurturing my relationships now and doing all I can to fulfil my purpose.

Going back to the issue of money, isn't it interesting that you may be slaving it out as a man to bring home 'the bacon' and after a while all your wife has to say to you is, "Honey, we haven't spent much time together lately; do you still love me?" The chances are that you may be offended or even furious. After all you are looking after the family's interests, but that may not be what the woman cherishes most at that point in time.

So if the best things in life are free, what are they with specific reference to marriage?

Friendship

Your spouse should be your friend, your very best friend. Dami discussed this in her chapter on 'Good Things Come to Those Who Wait.' You should not require gimmicks to be comfortable in each other's company. If all you do is have sex and you cannot have a meaningful conversation with each other, the future is not very bright for your relationship. Don't get me wrong; we had lots and lots of sex in the early days. We both got married as virgins so we were at it up to two or three times daily in the first year or two! I don't know where we got the energy from back then! But we were first and foremost friends and that costs nothing. We were and still are very comfortable in each other's company and are able to have decent meaningful conversations for hours on end. Friends hang out, go for a meal together, maybe even a movie which costs money but it is all based on a relationship between two individuals and that is free.

Now there is a type of cost though. It will cost you time and effort to build and develop your friendship and you will have to pay for gifts and outings to express your love for each other but the essence of your friendship will always be free. Steve Jobs said,

"My favourite things in life don't cost any money. It's really clear that the most precious resource we all have is time".

The early days might have been a bit challenging for us financially but they helped strengthen our marriage. We always had to be in the same room (remember the single electric heater), we had to do things together, communicate with each other, bath and shower together, eat together and sleep together.

Love

H. Jackson Brown Jr, the author of *Life's Little Instruction Book* defines love as 'when the other person's happiness is more important than your own'. I have always told Dami that one of my purposes in life is to make her happy.

I must share with you an important truth at this point though - no one can really make you happy. Being happy is a decision you have to take for yourself. We all have reasons to be unhappy. Life has happened to all of us and we could choose to wallow in our various reasons to be unhappy. One of the things that will make you happy, is choosing to be selfless in your marriage and prioritise your spouse's happiness over your own. In the Marriage Preparation Class where I serve, we call it 'Minding your own business'. Your business is to do what YOU should be doing in marriage and not complaining about what is not being done for you. If we all minded and took care of our business, business would be all taken care of.

What were your marriage vows? There is a good chance it went something like this: 'To have and to hold, to love and to cherish, forsaking all others and so on and so forth.' Well get on with it then! Show some love, show your spouse some love in a way they can appreciate that they are loved, in a manner they can comprehend they are loved, in a language they can understand they are loved.

Dr Gary Chapman in his book *'The Five Love Languages'* tells us there are five specific love languages, five means of communicating love. These are love languages in which we prefer to give and receive love in. They are:

- Words of affirmation - for people who feel love when you speak encouraging words to them

- Acts of service - for people who feel love when you do things for them

- Receiving gifts - for people who feel love when you buy things for them

- Quality time - for people who feel love when you spend time with them

- Physical touch - for people who feel love when you touch them

In order to effectively love your spouse you need to love them in the language THEY understand, not just the one you speak. It's interesting to note that all of the love languages apply to all of us to a certain degree but some are more significant than others. If you speak your spouse's love language you will succeed in making and keeping them happy. Apart from the receiving gifts, all the love languages are free to give and free to receive.

Romance

How is romance different from love you may ask? Then you might as well ask how is icing different from cake? Love is the cake of your relationship, the substance, the core, and the values on which it is based. Romance is the icing, the fun, the sweetness, the excitement. You may not always feel like your head is in the clouds but you should always love your spouse. Sometimes you feel tired or upset and there may be periods of ill health. Through all of that, you may not feel very romantic but you still love. Romance deals with the 'head in the clouds' bit.

Romance may be superficial but it is very sweet! It is the feeling of excitement that takes your friendship and love to a whole new plane. It is what you DO to SHOW you love someone. It is made up of the little things like hugging, kissing, holding each other's hands, gazing into each other's eyes, the cuddles and all the 'I love yous'. Things like sending cards, texts, poems, breakfast in bed, strolling in the park, tender moments, cooking a special dinner, in fact anything that makes your spouse feel special.

Relationships built mainly on romance are exciting, breath-taking and explosive even but they usually don't last. Relationships built on friendship and true love last forever but they can become boring without romance. Find love and friendship first (bake the cake), then introduce romance (add the icing).

We will all be guilty of taking our spouses for granted from time to time, making them feel like they will always be there. Many religious couples are guilty of this. As many religions do not endorse divorce, many may take their spouses for granted for this very reason.

When last did YOU make your spouse feel special? Do you even know how to make your spouse feel special? She knows you love her (in your own way) but when last did you make her feel special?

I call Dami at work every day. It is a connecting point for us. Her colleagues know that at a certain time after my morning surgery I will call. It makes her feel special. When we are sitting in church, I hold her hand or gently stroke her thigh; it makes her feel special. I ensure I speak her love language on a regular basis; that makes her feel special. It's not the big things like buying a nice house or a car. That's all good but you are going to live there too and drive the car with her. It's the little things that are for him or her alone. Remember, the best things in life are free.

Loyalty

One of my definitions for love is commitment. Till death do us part, richer or poorer, sickness or health. A famous actor Sylvester Stallone once said,

> *"I learned the real meaning of love. Love is absolute loyalty. People fade, looks fade but loyalty never fades. You can depend so much on certain people, you can set your watch by them. And that's love, even if it doesn't seem very exciting".*

Other words for loyalty include faithfulness, devotion, reliability and dependability. The issue of loyalty and commitment is sadly lacking in society today in which marriages are collapsing at the first sign of trouble. Everyone feels more loved, more at ease and more comfortable in a relationship in which they know without a doubt that their spouse is absolutely committed to them. We all need to look for little ways to show our loyalty and commitment.

Dami and I keep no secrets from each other. She knows the passwords to my phone, my email accounts, my laptop and we have a joint bank account. She knows where I am at every point in time. I call her every day after my morning surgery just to say 'Hi' and let her know what I am doing and what I will be doing next. She knows I am absolutely committed to her. Although I am very expressive with my affection anyway but even if I was not, my actions clearly show my loyalty to this relationship. Just this morning, while reviewing this chapter, she was out shopping and in a moment of brain block she forgot the pin to her debit card! She quickly called me and I was able to tell her because we know each other's personal identification numbers (PIN).

NO ONE comes before Dami. Not my friends, not my family, not even the children. Our daughters know mummy comes first and that they are an extremely close second. They already know that unless a man loves them the way their dad loves their mother, they have no business even considering him as a potential husband. Unless a man treats them the way their dad treats their mother, they won't even entertain him. In marriage, only absolute loyalty works. Anything short of that will cause problems in the future.

Chapter lessons:

- The best things in life are free like friendship, love, romance and loyalty.

- The presence of money cannot make you happier but the absence of money can make you miserable.

- Find out how to make your spouse feel special.

5
The Advantage of Adversity

All the adversity I've had in my life, all my troubles and obstacles, have strengthened me. You may not realize it when it happens, but a kick in the teeth may be the best thing in the world for you.
Walt Disney

Dami

One of the major lessons we have learnt in our marriage is that there is an advantage to every adversity. A few weeks before I wrote this chapter, Wole asked me what I would change in our lives if I had the opportunity. My husband can be very philosophical, so he comes up with these abstract questions from time to time, designed to make us think and reflect about our lives and relationships. I thought deeply at his question. We have had some torrid times in our lives: lost pregnancies (both of which almost resulted in my death), lost investments, friendship let downs, disappointments, initially unrealised dreams and aspirations. So I had lots to choose from! But the more I thought about it, the more I realised that whatever I had lost as a result of my adversity, had become an advantage in my marriage and my life as a whole.

Take the pregnancies that I lost for example. Those experiences made me the person I am today. I have become a major resource for women who have had difficulty in pregnancy or childbirth as a direct result of my experiences. No matter what the women have been through, hearing my story makes many of them realise 'you can come back from the brink'.

The adverse experiences were invaluable for our marriage. The commitment and loyalty which Wole demonstrated to me during those very dark periods was second to none. He was a rock for me. I felt secure enough to cry openly with him, tell him my deepest fears, open up my vulnerabilities and he never once used any of them against me. The strength that feeling of security brought to me and our marriage was colossal. The implicit trust and respect I developed for him as a result has been a bedrock in our relationship.

Every adversity you go through as a couple will either strengthen your marriage or weaken it. If things are not well handled, adversity can even break your marriage apart. There are certain things you need to put in place in your marriage that will ensure that whatever adversity you face becomes an advantage. I will encapsulate them under the 4 Cs.

Conviction

This is a crucial element in turning your adversity into a marital advantage. You should have a strong conviction that you should be married to your spouse in the first place. For some superstitious or religious folk, negative occurrences are a sign that you are in the wrong place. When things go wrong, as they sometimes do in life, you need to be able to stand together in support of each other. I have heard too many stories of people battling illness only for the spouse to walk. One of the first things my pastor asked us to do when we started seeing each other was to write down our conviction(s). Why do you feel you should be married to this person?

That was easy for me as I had a very spiritual experience which formed the bedrock of my conviction to get married to Wole. I have a gift in that my dreams tend to more or less come to pass. Before Wole and I became friends, I had a dream in which he introduced me as the woman he wanted to marry to his parents and three siblings. Many months later I realised how accurate my dream was when I realised he had two sisters and a brother which I had not known before. In addition to that, he ticked the boxes on my list so my conviction was firm.

Wole had no problems writing his convictions either. He was reflecting and praying on a particular day when he felt a strong urge to pray against anything that would stand against my marriage to him. The interesting thing was that at this point we were just friends! He wasn't particularly thinking about marriage at that time either. He tells me that he had started to 'zero in on me' as one of the female friends he could possibly end up with and he had admitted to himself that he really liked me. From that point he started to match my qualities to the things he wanted in a wife and he found that I ticked all the boxes that were important to him. With convictions as strong as ours, we absolutely know that we belong together. We absolutely want to be together and when things are not going well, we are absolutely committed to fight for our marriage.

'Good relationships don't just happen. They take time, patience and two people who truly want to be together'. Author unknown

Irrespective of what we have been through as a couple, our belief that we should be together, our desire to want to be together makes us pull out the stops to make things work.

Communication

For your adversity to become an advantage you need to communicate. Communication is about effective speaking and effective listening. You both need an opportunity to express how you feel but also to listen to how the situation is making your spouse feel. In this, you support each other through your adversity. We refer to this as 'emotional unpacking'. Opening up your fears and vulnerabilities about your adversity will make you closer and more dependent on each other as a couple.

Having dealt with the emotion of your adversity, you will also need to communicate your thoughts about the situation and then go through the process of discussing what you will do about it. This is the 'practical unpacking'. This involves assessing the adversity, discussing how it has affected you practically and planning and working together on what to do next. All of this involves spending time together. If you notice, there are lots of 'together' in what needs to be done which is the basis of a strong relationship. Doing things together is the lifeline of a marriage that will last and weather the storms of life.

Counsel

This can be very useful if you are feeling very overwhelmed by what you are going through. It is very important that you agree on who you approach for counsel. You can seek counsel from at least three sets of people.

- **Experienced people**: These are those who have been through what you are experiencing and are able to give you practical advice on how they coped. As a result of my experience with the pregnancies that I lost, I have become a resource for ladies who have similar experiences either at church or at work. On several occasions I have been asked to speak to ladies who were inconsolable after the experience of a lost pregnancy. Once they hear my story, they often forget about their problems thinking: 'if you went through that and came out the other side, there is hope for me!'

- **Professional people**: These are those who are professionally skilled and have acquired the relevant expertise to give you the right sort of advice on specific matters. These could be medical professionals or financial experts depending on the sort of situation you find yourself in.

- **Counsellors**: These are people who are either professional counsellors or leaders in society such as religious organisations who can give you guidance and direction. They serve as a resource for you to unburden your emotions if you feel extra support is required. They can also give practical advice on managing anxiety, and may sometimes ask you to see your General Practitioner if they are concerned you have become overwhelmed to the point of feeling depressed.

Just a couple of extra notes on this point of counsel. A spouse who has no one in his or her life who can speak to him or her is a dangerous person. We should all be humble enough to accept counsel from those who know better. If you are too proud to listen to others, at some point you will refuse to listen to your spouse which will result in conflict. You should as much as possible have a friendly couple that BOTH of you respect and honour enough to allow them to speak into your lives. This will ensure that irrational decisions are not made when you are under pressure to the detriment of your relationship. Many marriages have been damaged as a result of failing to ensure good counsel in the marriage. However I must sound a note of warning: you are BOTH responsible for ensuring who you get good counsel from.

Composition

This is a very important aspect in dealing with adversity and challenging situations. Composition refers to your make up, your mind-set, your personality and what makes you, you. You are the sum of your knowledge, experiences, likes and dislikes, and everything about you. The likelihood is that you and your spouse deal with things differently. What might not be a big deal to you might be stuff of the legendary Armageddon to your spouse! Be patient with their concerns. Being self-aware will help you determine what you are better dealing with.

There is the possibility that one of you will have a calm head and the other will be fiery. One may be more rational and the other more emotional. Both personality types are important in turning your adversity to advantage. In any situation, a particular composition may be better suited to seeing things more clearly. Whoever that is should take the lead. For example when we lost the pregnancies, Wole being less emotional and more mature spiritually was able to take the lead. He reassured and encouraged me and helped me to see the advantage in our adversity. But at the time, I couldn't see the advantages, I was more concerned about the losses.

I remember one day I was crying, wondering why life was being so tough to me. Many other ladies I know who were pregnant at the same time had their babies and I felt so dejected. Wole reminded me how fortunate we were. All other areas of our lives were functioning exactly as we wanted. He reminded me that it was only a matter of time and we would soon have another baby. He reminded me of how close we had become as a couple which strengthened our marriage. He told me that one day, we would have a story to tell that would help many people. He was right!

Though I would not want the pain and trauma of such an experience again, I have to admit that one of the reasons we are so close today was the dark seasons we faced together. I also have to admit that one of the reasons women listen to me today is that I have experienced their pain and even worse. When we had issues with lost investments however and were financially affected, I took the lead as I deal more with money matters and management in the home. Wole does not like dealing with the day-to-day running of the accounts and bills. Although we discussed it, I executed the plans.

No one prays for adversity; they come anyway. The

winds of life will blow. We are to hope for the best in life but also to prepare for the worst. The old parable Jesus told of building your house on the rock rather than on the sand holds very true here. By putting in place a strong conviction, good communication, mature counsel and understanding our individual compositions, we are laying a strong foundation on which to build our marriage that will turn any adversity to an advantage.

Chapter lessons:

- Every adversity can become an advantage to your marriage if you have the right ingredients in place.

- Strengthen your conviction. This should be ideally done BEFORE marriage but can also be done after.

- Learn the value in emotional and practical unpacking TOGETHER.

- Have a mature couple with a great marriage that YOU BOTH RESPECT who you can turn to for advice.

- Recognise the value of your differences in dealing with adversity and use those differences in a complementary manner.

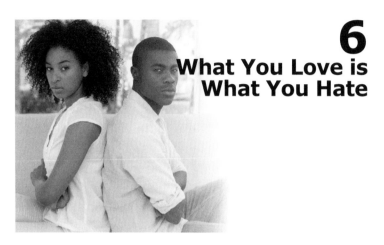

6
What You Love is What You Hate

There are two sides to every coin. English idiom

Wole

A coin has two sides. This English idiom helps us to understand the fact that two things can be closely related, inseparable and intertwined but also different. Understanding this concept can be a great help in dealing with differences in your marriage. There are two main ways in which this can help. The first is that it helps you to appreciate that the negative things you hate about your spouse are actually the other side of the coin of the positive things you like about your spouse. The second is that knowing about the two sides of a coin can be useful in recognising that we have different gifts and abilities which should be used in a complementary manner.

The other side of the coin

Dami is a focussed, driven, principled and disciplined woman. She is a keen homemaker who is very house proud. She does all the washing, ironing and cleaning herself and even used to do the gardening as well. She is very much into house maintenance and keeps everything in the house running smoothly. If an appliance is not functioning well, she will start to discuss its replacement or repair. She looks after the children and helps them with their homework and helps them develop good moral values. She ensures our daughters have very nice clothes and look great at home and when we go out. She is a very attractive woman who looks after herself very well, dresses impeccably and decently at all times. She is perfectly manicured and looks nowhere near her age. I find her very sexy. She is the perfect ideal wife and I consider myself HIGHLY BLESSED to have her as mine. As she does the laundry, she knows when my shirts need changing and 90 per cent of all my clothes were bought by her.

On a rating scale, I would struggle to mark her as excellent as that does not even start to qualify her. I don't do comparisons but no one I know has a woman quite like mine. I haven't even begun to talk about her commitment to social causes like the development of women and children, her passion to see marriages and families established, and I could go on and on.

Living with and being married to such a wonderful individual must be absolutely fantastic you think. She takes care of so much that you have very little to worry about. I agree but consider the flip side of the very same coin. Her being focussed, driven and principled means she can often be a kill joy. Things need to be done at specific times and everything has to be arranged in a specific way. Sometimes, just when the children and I want to settle down to watch a movie, she reminds them of the outstanding homework they had promised to do! Being house proud means everywhere (and I mean EVERYWHERE) has to be spic and span ALL THE TIME! What a bother! Washing up must be done after each and every meal, no plates must be left in the sink (who does that?!).

Dami can also sometimes be a nag if what can be done tomorrow was not done yesterday! Since she works very hard (she still works three days a week in addition to all of the above) sometimes at night (or early morning), she is too tired for 'you know what'. What a pain! House maintenance means we end up spending lots of money on top quality things as only the best will do. In addition to that, it is not cheap for a family to dress in good quality clothes.

Now I have a choice. I can focus on all the things I 'hate' about her which will result in lots of arguments and disputes as we are quite different in a great number of things; or I can focus on the things I love about her, realising that what I love and what I hate are just two sides of the same coin.

I have found this principle works with every couple

that I have had the privilege of interacting with. In the Marriage Enrichment Team we belong to, we often test out this theory on those who attend the Marriage Preparation Program. We ask an individual to say what they love most about their spouse's nature (not physical looks or appearance) and we can then 'predict' by simply flipping the coin what annoys or irritates them most about their spouse as well. It never fails! For example if you like the fact that your spouse is gentle and easy going, the likelihood is that you will be irritated by the fact that they take their time doing things or arriving at decisions. If what you like about them is their drive and determination to get things done against the odds, I am also certain you will be irritated by the fact that they can be nags.

A deeper analysis of the exact dynamics here reveals that the things I 'hate' about my spouse are probably areas of life in which I am not able to keep up with my spouse, areas of life in which I feel I am inadequate.

If you analyse the things I 'hate' about Dami such as her being disciplined, extremely clean and tidy, spending lots of money on the family and the house, they are areas in which I am less comfortable. I am a big picture person, not into small details, I am certainly not as clean and tidy, and I like making money but not spending it!

Why do we quarrel?

We quarrel with our spouses when areas in which we feel less adequate are brought to light. Basically, areas in which we feel insecure or uncomfortable. We feel exposed, our weaknesses are being highlighted, and our deficiencies are being made to take centre stage so our natural response is to go on the offensive or to retreat depending on our personality types.

In the early years of our marriage, a major bug bear for us was the whole issue of keeping the house clean and washing up. There are certain things I feel I have done enough of in my life time and one of them happens to be washing up. Dami likes the sink kept clean and empty at all times. Her view is 'if you use it, wash it up.' My view is, 'if you use it, leave it in the sink for washing later if someone else hasn't done it first!' The fact that she was always nagging me about it made me feel inadequate about my level of tidiness and cleanliness compared to her.

Dami would describe me as a 'cool guy', laid back, easy going, always happy as Larry, always seeing the positive in everything. She loves the fact that I am passionate about my work as a GP and love helping people. What she 'hates' about me is that I could be seen as not taking life too seriously since I do things in my own time. I could also be considered to enjoy chilling out a bit too much but can sometimes be over committed to my work or to church activities in my bid to be helpful to other people. She could either focus on the positive aspects of my nature or the negative expressions of it. Clearly two sides of the same coin.

Compete and Complement

The second way in which knowing about the two sides can be useful is recognising that we have different gifts and abilities. She is good at something I am not and I can do certain things well that she cannot. This is true in most marriage relationships; you will be good at something your spouse is not and vice-versa. We touched on this slightly in the last chapter under composition.

The two sides of a person are 'a good side' and 'a not so good' side depending on your view point, but for you as a couple working together, it becomes a good side and another good side! You protect each other's weaknesses by keeping them hidden from public view and exposed only to each other. Like two coins placed together, the sides facing each other will be your theoretical weak sides with your strengths facing the outside.

At this point you come to a place where your virtues become complementary of each other; you recognise each other's strengths and you work with your strengths as a couple. Learn to see your strengths as complementary, two coins fused together with their better sides facing up and their weaker sides kept in, away from view.

Chapter lessons:

- What I hate (dislike) about my spouse is simply the other side of the coin of what I like about him/her. Therefore, I must be more understanding as I cannot have one without the other.

- I must be careful about making my spouse feel inadequate in areas where I am strong.

- I must be careful about making myself feel inadequate in areas where I am weak.

- Our different abilities are complementary not contradictory and certainly not for competing against each other.

7
Sex is Food for Men (and Women Too!)

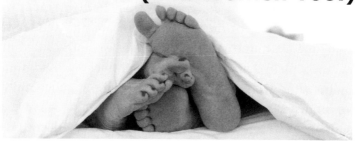

Sex is as important as eating and drinking and we ought to allow the one appetite to be satisfied with as little restraint or false modesty as the other. Marquis de Sade

Women need a reason to have sex, men just need a place.
Billy Crystal

Dami

We were in our mid-twenties when we got married and we were both virgins. (It can be done if you want to!) There was great anticipation. We had promised ourselves and the Lord that we would wait and we did. No hanky-panky, no slip ups, no lines crossed. Those were our Christian values and we kept to it. The moment we got married we hit the sheets (sorry ground!) running. It was a little awkward getting things rolling on our wedding night as we were both a bit shy and embarrassed (Wole more than me!), but once we did, it was plain sailing from there. It was beautiful.

For the first three months of marriage we had sex more or less twice daily. Wole then had to travel to England as part of our plan to relocate and we were apart for six months. It was difficult for both of us but we soon picked up where we left off once I joined him. By the time we had been having sex about twice daily for almost two years I was getting to the point of having enough. I started to make up excuses and we started to fall out a lot over the issue of sex.

One day Wole was talking yet again about the insufficient quality and quantity of sex and I asked my now famous question, "Is sex food?" His answer was, "Yes it is! It is food for me!" Hence the title of this chapter, 'Sex is food'.

Most men like sex and they like it a lot. They want as much of it as they can, as often as they can; they are like ever ready batteries. They would certainly agree with Marquis de Sade's view on sex: no restraint! Once you start to peel off your clothes to change in front of them, they are ready. You pull down your panties to use the toilet and the sight of your bare bottom springs them into action. You lie in bed with them simply wanting a cuddle and you start to feel something hard pressing on you; come on!

Lots of research has been conducted to ascertain how much men and women think about sex. It was banded about that men think about sex every seven seconds which is almost impossible and has been proven not to be true. Current research puts it at anything from every 30 to 90 mins but almost all studies place men thinking about sex twice as often as women do on average.

This statistic will roughly equate to men wanting sex twice as often as women and this can be a source of conflict in marriage as it was in ours. I started to feel very inadequate about satisfying my husband's needs until I started speaking to other women. I realised we were all having the same problem and I felt reassured that I was normal for not wanting sex as often as Wole did but I also realised however that he was also normal for wanting sex as often as he did. So what was the solution?

Communication and understanding

By now you would have realised that you cannot get away from communication in marriage. It is the life blood of your marriage and indeed of any relationship. When communicating about sex, what exactly should be the subject of your discussion? These are a few suggestions from our experience:

Why do we have sex?

This is an interesting question. Why do we have sex? For many couples, the answer to this question is: 'To keep the man happy'. But in reality sex is food for men AND women. It may not be food women want to 'eat' as often as men do but it is important nonetheless. If your reason for having sex is only ever to keep one person happy, that may have issues of its own that need to be dealt with. Remember marriage is for both of you. You should be having sex to express your love for each other and also to satisfy your natural sexual needs. Men function better when they have been 'sexed up' but women should not be having sex only for the sake of the men. There are multiple health benefits directly associated with sex which we will see later in this chapter.

What does it mean (to us) to have good sex?

What would be the markers of a good session of sex? This would be a very interesting discussion. A good session of Hollywood sex or pornographic sex is very different from real sex in the real world. Do you know of any of your friends who rip of their clothes any time they want to hit the sheets? This is the time to share together what we really want from each other when it comes to sex. A frank discussion will be an opportunity to expose unrealistic expectations.

Obviously climaxing is extremely important, but how do you want to get there? How do you want to be taken there? What do you enjoy most? Is foreplay adequate? It is possible to climax and feel like you arrived at your destination but you did not quite enjoy the journey.

What is allowed?

This discussion is to ensure that no party feels compelled to engage in any form of sexual activity they are uncomfortable with. You both have to be clear about what is allowed and not allowed in your marriage. Following our research into this, the general rule and consensus is that as long as you are both comfortable with your sexual practices as a couple then it is fine. However, if what you are both comfortable with is socially unacceptable or deviant then you need to check your practices. Things like paedophilia and bestiality are completely unacceptable.

Who will be involved?

This might sound like a question with an obvious answer but it will surprise you the number of people who strongly entertain thoughts of extra marital affairs, threesomes and 'moresomes' for whatever reason. Having this discussion might reveal a treasure trove of information and may pre-empt actions that would prove to be costly to your marriage later. We believe that only the two of you as a married couple should be sexually involved.

Which positions should we adopt?

Over time, couples become accustomed to certain routine sexual positions. This discussion will aim to broaden your experience to experiment a bit more within the confines of what you are both comfortable with.

When will we be having it?

If you have different biological clocks this could be an issue. Some prefer night, some prefer day. Others don't mind either. If you keep trying to have sex when one party is asleep then some wires are getting crossed.

Where will we be having it?

Bedroom, bathroom, sitting room, kitchen, all of the above, or none of the above! Some couples are not able to have sex in their house due to living with friends and relatives.

How often will we be having it?

This is probably the major bone of contention when it comes to sex. Leaving this to chance will not be productive. The average from available studies is two to three times weekly but the important thing is to agree on what is right and appropriate for your relationship. The more you agree on in this area, the less likely you are to have issues. There will be no need for wandering eyes or infidelity if you are happy with your sex lives as a couple.

While I was reviewing this chapter, one of my aunts who also serves in the Marriage Enrichment Team at my church, sent us an article taken from a book called 'Because it feels good: a woman's guide to sexual pleasure and satisfaction' by Debby Herbenick. Apparently, scientists have discovered that there are multiple health benefits to having early morning sex at least three times a week. It builds your immune system, reduces the risk of catching colds, lessens your chances of getting strokes or heart attacks and is a good stress buster which helps with depression. So if you want to live a healthy, stress free, cancer free, stroke free and heart attack free life, have sex at least three times weekly!

No Go Areas of Sex

Sex is a beautiful thing when two people in a loving and committed marriage relationship give themselves to each other. However like anything good, sex can be abused. We want to mention a few ways that sex can be abused in a relationship.

- Sex should not be used as a reward, and should not be withheld as punishment.

- Sex should not be obtained by bullying or beating, which is rape even in a marriage relationship.

- Sex should not be used to ridicule your spouse either with respect to size (of genitals), sexual performance or ability.

- Sex should not be engaged in if there are unresolved issues, but unresolved issues should not be used as an excuse not to have sex. Resolve the issues!

Intimacy

Having discussed sex, let us look into the subject of intimacy. Men need to understand that although sex is food for them, intimacy is more our kind of meal and intimacy is not the same as sex for many women. Although women do like and enjoy sex, we prefer intimacy. So what is the difference?

Intimacy refers to the close, familiar and affectionate relationship that exists between a couple. It is the state of being emotionally close to your partner, being able to let your guard down, and being able to let him or her know how you really feel.

When a woman feels intimately close to a man she is more likely to have sex with him because she feels safe, secure and open. The animalistic ripping off of clothes that is sometimes portrayed in movies is so unreal unless both have been significantly sex-starved. And also, it cannot be mutually satisfying as they are both going at it with raw, unbridled primitive sexual desire. Sex born out of intimacy is usually preceded by emotional warmth, cuddling, discussions about how you feel about each other, petting, openness and the nakedness both of the soul and of the body. The latter results in sex which is affectionate, caring and satisfying.

For this reason, it is difficult to comprehend having an extremely close relationship with a member of the opposite sex who is not your spouse. If you are that close, then you are becoming emotionally intimate and that can lead to physical intimacy. So it is like 'playing with fire' for a man or a woman to become emotionally close to someone they are not espoused to.

Communication about intimacy and your sex lives should happen freely and frequently. Intimacy and the act of sexual intercourse are in themselves forms of communication. You can either be communicating love, lust, care, aggression, selfishness or even depravity. Not having sex is also communicating something. For an unmarried couple, it could be communicating commitment to each other's values of 'no sex before marriage', or for a married couple it could be communicating the absence of intimacy. What are you communicating when you have sex with your spouse?

Chapter lessons:

- Sex is food for both men and women but women prefer intimacy.

- Copious communication about intimacy and sex should happen freely and frequently.

- Men will on average want sex twice as much as their wives.

- Sex is a form of communication. What will a study of your sex lives over the past few months tell us about your marriage?

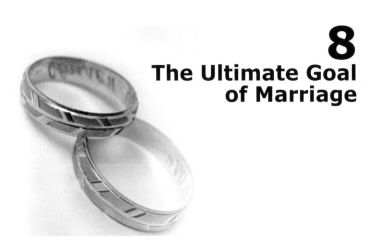

8
The Ultimate Goal
of Marriage

Therefore shall a man leave his father and his mother, and shall cleave unto his wife: and they shall be one flesh. The Bible

Wole & Dami

Many marriage recitals will include the phrase above from the Bible which refers to the man and his wife becoming one flesh. We believe the goal of marriage is oneness: two people from different backgrounds, different perspectives, merging together to become one.

True marriage is not co-habitation

Co-habitation is not just two people living together without being married but could also be two people who may have a marriage license but are not merging their lives together. True marriage is oneness. The more united you are, the more things you agree on as a couple. The more integrated your lives are, the more at one you are, the more difficult it becomes to allow external interference in your marriage relationship.

Every marriage is on a journey; the goal of that journey is to achieve oneness. That journey will take you through at least three phases, each with its own characteristics. None of the developmental phases are bad in themselves depending on how long you have been married. The three phases are found in the passage above: leaving, cleaving and oneness.

Leaving

Marriages in this phase are dealing with external influences. It is clear that for your marriage to be successful you need to 'LEAVE'. In the first few years of marriage you are still very much connected to previous influences such as family, friends, work and maybe even previous relationships. Now that you are married or as you progress towards marriage, your loyalties should start to change. This does not mean you will stop associating with everyone and anyone you had in your life before, but it does mean they should no longer take centre stage. Clear boundaries need to be introduced to ensure the marriage is allowed to thrive.

Some married folk still have very strong parental ties. Their parents still have a say in everything that happens in their home and this can create resentment. Many mothers are reluctant to let go of their sons and end up trying to compete with their daughter-in-law. It is the responsibility of every spouse to protect their marriage from their own family.

Now this must not be misunderstood. We must be very appreciative of our parents. Many of them have gone through many sacrifices to help get us to where we are. For the most part they only want what is best for us and are trying to be protective of their 'little babies'. However, for a marriage to thrive, there does need to be a 'leaving' in order to prevent external interference and this means nicely but firmly ensuring appropriate boundaries.

We have been given permission to share the example of a couple who were having some difficulty in this area. We will call them Pau and Cimy (not their real names). Pau was extremely close to his mother and made every decision regarding his nuclear family with his mother as the main factor. His decisions on where to live, where the children schooled and even things to do with their marriage were all determined by what his mum's opinion or preferences were. Cimy had always expressed concern about his decisions and gradually started to feel more and more like an appendage in her own marriage. Unfortunately, things did not improve and the couple ended up separating. The real problem here was the lack of boundary setting from the beginning. There was too much external interference from Pau's mother which resulted in the marriage collapsing. The process of 'leaving' is therefore very important.

Some couples have friends that are closer than their spouses. This should not be the case under normal circumstances. Some even have friends of the opposite sex that are closer than their spouses, which can get complicated as it can lead to emotional ties to others apart from your spouse. You can have best friends you talk to and sometimes confide in but they should not be higher on the scale than your spouse. A good best friend will always encourage your relationship with your spouse over your relationship with them.

Some have ex-boyfriends or ex-girlfriends (or ex-husbands/wives) that are still very close and sometimes closer than their spouses. This can be a little complicated especially if you have children together. You need to maintain a good relationship not just for the sake of the children but also to promote your own healing. However, if you find yourself preferring the company of your ex-partner to that of your spouse then clear boundaries need to be introduced. This is someone you were (and maybe still are) attracted to and there has to be a clear 'leaving'. By all means maintain an amicable relationship but your spouse comes first.

Cleaving

Marriages in this phase are dealing with internal forces. Many people have lived their lives in one way or another for a number of years before marriage. There is a manner in which you do things, see things and decide on things. All of a sudden you get married and someone else starts to introduce their views, their say and their decisions. Wait a minute!

Cleaving refers to progressive synchronisation. The process of becoming inseparable, merged, fused and amalgamated. This can be a traumatic process which is why conflict is so important, so necessary and so useful. Every discussion or dispute is important. Every time you gently confront each other and express your differences with the resultant effect of coming to a shared common understanding, you are cleaving. Your marriage gradually comes to a place of unity across all the decasections (10 sections) of your life.

That's why the manner in which you conduct your disputes can either make you feel loved or make you feel slighted. It is important to fight fair. No shouting, no insulting, no threats, just good wholesome communication. Every good and kind word you say regarding the marriage promotes cleaving. Every unresolved conflict pulls you apart. Simone Signoret once said,

> *"Chains do not hold a marriage together. It is threads, hundreds of tiny threads which sew people together through the years."*

Those tiny threads are the little things like the kind words, thoughtful deeds, and times of intimacy. The fights and unresolved disputes cut the threads away. Focus on promoting cleaving for a strong healthy marriage.

Oneness

Marriages in this phase are dealing with progressive unity. This is when the synchronisation process is reaching its full potential. People asking you questions get the same answer from both of you. You have understood each other's mindsets, thought processes and viewpoints. It is more than knowing each other; you are becoming each other in a wholesome non-domineering way.

As we were approaching our tenth year in marriage, we started to feel there was something missing. We had a good relationship, we got on well with each other, we had learned to fight fair and resolve conflicts amicably, things were going well but we still felt something was missing. One day, we were listening to a lecture by an influential American cleric and coach (Dr A.R. Bernard) when he asked the question, "What is the goal of marriage?" Lots of answers were given: friendship, children, sex, society, and he simply responded, "The goal of marriage is oneness".

Immediately, we looked at each other and smiled. We had found the missing piece, the focus we would have for the rest of our lives: oneness.

Oneness refers to unity, togetherness, cohesion and agreement. Henry Ford said,

> *"Coming together is a beginning. Keeping together is progress. Working together is success"*

A successful marriage is one in which you have come

together (leaving), kept together (cleaving) and are working together (oneness). We took a decision about eight years ago to walk in complete and total unity and agreement with a view to further strengthen our marriage and help us achieve oneness. Anything we do not agree on, does not happen. We apply this to even simple things such as furniture and household items like televisions or vacuum cleaners. Since we take all significant decisions together, there is no room for blame as we are both responsible!

We were due to change our TV some years ago but because we could not agree on exactly what we wanted, we stayed with the old one. The old one was our first TV together bought in 1999! Could we afford a new TV? Yes, but because we had not agreed on exactly what we wanted, we did not buy one. We were at a shopping centre one day, shopping for something else and we saw this TV. We looked at each other and smiled. We bought it that same day. We found something we agreed on and we went for it. We apply this principle to everything. There is great power in unity. The Bible says, "Two people are better off than one, for they can help each other succeed. If one person falls, the other can reach out and help. But someone who falls alone is in real trouble".

You are better together. Sometimes it does not feel like it. Some of you reading this book may be having a difficult time in your marriage right now. You feel tempted to leave and pack it all in. You are both good people but with different viewpoints on life. Don't throw it all away. Seek good counsel and advice. Find people who can help you work through your differences. Agree to progress towards unity and enjoy the blissful marriage you were designed to have.

Chapter lessons:

- If you are still dealing with external forces, then you need more 'leaving'.

- If you are still dealing with internal forces, then you need more 'cleaving'.

- The goal of marriage is oneness. Seek to become progressively more and more united and to operate in togetherness and agreement.

- Whatever stage of marriage you are in, seek to progress higher.

Conclusion

Marriage is a life long journey which is hard work, but well worth the investment. When it goes wrong, the consequences can be devastating but when it goes well, the rewards can be exhilarating.

One way to ensure that you get to your destination hitch free is to follow the map and guidance of those who have gone ahead of you and are making a good job of it.

As we celebrate 18 years of marriage, we still consider ourselves young adults of marriage, but we are walking a very good path and we hope our practical tips will prove useful for you as they have for us and many others whom we have had personal contact with.

We know you may have questions to ask and we would be delighted if you got in touch with us via our website **www.decasections.org.**

We wish you every blessing!

Wole and Dami

March 2016

Another Book from Decasections.org

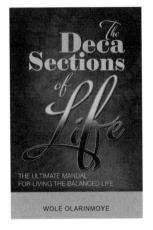

The Decasections of Life

Author: Wole Olarinmoye

ISBN-13: 978-1-908588-10-4

Format: Paperback, Pages: 168

Book information

Do you sometimes feel deficient in one or more areas of your life? Do you feel that there is more to life than you are currently experiencing? Have you ever wondered if there were certain boxes in your life you are not yet ticking? Are you aware that there are at least ten areas of your life which all need attention? Have you ever thought about how the different parts of your life link up?

Inside *The Decasections of Life,* Wole explains that real success is only achieved when you are successful in all ten areas of your life. He breaks down each area of life and asks insightful questions throughout the book that will provoke you to reflect on your life, setting you on the path to true success. Once you start reading The Decasections of Life, you will see life differently and start to grasp everything that belongs to you. You cannot be the same again!

Here to help

We have written *Marriage Lessons* as a service to this generation. We have shared our own experience from when we were single, and of working together as a couple over the years pursuing busy and demanding careers and raising godly children. We hope you have found it useful for whatever stage you're at. However, if you still have questions about your relationship, preparing for marriage, or about anything you have read in this book, you can contact us by email or via our website, www.decasections.org; we would be more than willing to answer your questions.

We look forward to hearing from you.

Wole and Dami Olarinmoye

www.decasections.org
info@decasections.org

Notes

Notes